THE SCIENCE OF
AIR

PROJECTS AND EXPERIMENTS WITH AIR AND FLIGHT

TABLETOP SCIENTIST

STEVE PARKER

Heinemann
LIBRARY

CONTENTS

The air which makes our weather…

…is measured using scientific devices…

…and holds up airplanes too, so we can fly around the world. Air also fills our car and bike tyres. Without air, we'd have a bumpy ride (and anyway, we'd be dead).

INTRODUCTION

Look all around you, and what can you see? Not air, even though it *is* all around you! Air is invisible. When we 'see' it, we are really seeing particles floating in it, like dust or water droplets. Or we are seeing its effects when it moves and blows, as the wind. Air might seem too light to have any weight. But it can be weighed, and it presses on us with a surprisingly powerful force. Of course, without air there would be no wind, clouds or weather. Air is even inside you. We must all breathe fresh air every few seconds, to stay alive. Scientists describe air as 'a mixture of gases forming a compressible fluid' – that is, air can flow and be squeezed smaller. Our scientific understanding of air means we can move it, push it, squash it, stretch it, alter it, measure it, and use it in countless ways, every day.

HOW IT WORKS

These panels explain the scientific ideas on which each project is based, and the processes that make it work.

Prepare each project carefully and follow the instructions. Remember: real scientists always put safety first.

TRY IT AND SEE

These panels show further ideas to try, so you can experiment and find out more about air.

Where you see these symbols:

 Ask an adult to help you.

 Project to be done outdoors.

 Sharp tools may be needed.

 Prepare work surface for a messy project.

AIR ON THE GO

Hot-air balloons contain air warmed by a burner. It's lighter than the surrounding cooler air, so the balloon takes off.

Air is rarely still. The layer of air around the whole Earth, called the atmosphere, is always on the move. It is heated by the Sun and parts of it get less dense, or lighter. A 'bubble' of warmer air rises above the cooler air around it. Some of this cooler air flows along to take its place – and so winds blow across the surface of the Earth.

PROJECT: BUILD A WIND CHIMNEY

Wind can be refreshing, but too much is damaging.

WIND CHIMNEY

WHAT YOU NEED

- **large plastic bottle**
- **thick card**
- **cooking foil**
- **cotton thread**
- **drinking straw**
- **bead**
- **glue**
- **craft knife**

1 CAREFULLY TRIM THE TOP AND BOTTOM FROM A LARGE PLASTIC FIZZY-DRINK BOTTLE. AT ONE END, CUT OUT TWO SQUARE SHAPES, OPPOSITE EACH OTHER.

2 CUT A CIRCLE OF COOKING FOIL TO FIT INSIDE THE BOTTLE. TRIM AWAY TWO QUARTER-SEGMENTS. TWIST THE REMAINING SEGMENTS TO MAKE A FAN SHAPE.

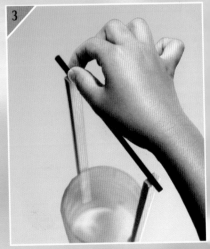

3 GLUE TWO LONG CARD STRIPS OPPOSITE EACH OTHER, AT THE OTHER END OF THE CHIMNEY TO THE CUTOUTS. GLUE THE STRAW ACROSS THEIR ENDS.

UPS AND DOWNS

As air warms its tiny particles, called atoms and molecules, move farther apart. There are fewer of them in a certain volume, so the warm air is lighter, or less dense, and moves upward. In the atmosphere, it is colder at great height. So the air cools, becomes heavier, and sinks. This sets up a continual flow called atmospheric circulation.

PLASTIC BOTTLE CHIMNEY

RISING HOT AIR

FOIL SHAPE

AIR

HOT AIR RISES

SUN HEATS GROUND AND AIR

HEAT SOURCE

HIGH UP, AIR COOLS AND SINKS

COOL AIR MOVES TO REPLACE HOT AIR

4

MAKE A SMALL HOLE IN THE MIDDLE OF THE FOIL. TIE ONE END OF THE COTTON TO THE BEAD. THREAD THE OTHER END THROUGH THE HOLE IN THE FOIL AND TIE IT TO THE STRAW.

TOWER POWER

ADJUST THE COTTON SO THE FOIL 'FAN' HANGS NEAR THE BASE. PUT THE CHIMNEY NEAR WARM AIR, FROM A RADIATOR, HOT-WATER BOTTLE OR SUNNY WINDOW. THE WARM AIR RISES UP THE CHIMNEY, PUSHES THE BLADES AND MAKES THEM SPIN. SCIENTISTS ARE PLANNING REAL 'SOLAR CHIMNEYS' ON HOT DESERT SAND, TO MAKE ELECTRICITY. THESE CHIMNEYS WILL BE OVER 1,000 METRES HIGH.

How windy?

How windy is it today? Is there a gentle breeze or a howling hurricane? Weather scientists, or meteorologists, need to know the detailed direction and speed of the wind. To measure these features they use a wind vane and anemometer.

The wind spins the cups of this portable anemometer, giving a digital read-out.

PROJECT: MAKE A WINDSPEED METER

WINDSPEED METER

What you need

- stiff card
- small tube
- thin dowel
- thick dowel
- string
- table-tennis ball
- drawing pin
- glue
- scissors

1 CUT A LARGE QUARTER-CIRCLE OF CARD. GLUE A THIN DOWEL ALONG ONE STRAIGHT EDGE.

2 GLUE THE CARD TUBE TO THE OTHER EDGE. TAPE CARD OVER THE TUBE END IN THE CORNER.

3 GLUE A CARD TRIANGLE TO THE TAIL OF THE DOWEL. THIS IS THE WIND VANE.

4 PUSH A DRAWING PIN INTO THE CORNER OF THE CARD'S NON-TUBE SIDE. GLUE ONE END OF THE STRING TO THE TABLE-TENNIS BALL. TIE THE OTHER TO THE PIN.

5 DRAW EVENLY-SPACED LINES ALONG THE CARD'S CURVED EDGE. FIX THE THICK DOWEL INTO THE GROUND SOMEWHERE WINDY. SLIDE THE TUBE OVER IT.

6 CHECK THE TABLE-TENNIS BALL SWINGS FREELY ALONG THE WINDSPEED SCALE AND THE WHOLE ANEMOMETER SWIVELS AROUND EASILY ON THE DOWEL.

THE PUSH OF THE WIND

As the wind's speed rises, the table-tennis ball is pushed higher up the scale. Put numbers on the scale and take measurements regularly through the day. If the wind is gusty (variable), try to get an average reading over, say, 10 seconds.

FACE THE WIND

The moving air pushes on the broad, flat surface of the wind vane and makes it turn. It swivels until the wind's force on it is least – when it points directly downwind. In this position the anemometer's table-tennis ball faces directly into the wind, and so the push of the moving air is greatest.

WIND VANE

WIND

TABLE-TENNIS BALL

BE A 'WINDBREAK'. STAND ON THE UPWIND SIDE OF THE ANEMOMETER. DOES THIS CHANGE THE READING?

HEAVY PRESSURE

All substances have weight, even air. Its weight presses on everything, including our bodies. But we are so used to it that we do not feel it. The pushing force of air is known as air pressure.

The pressure of the air around us is known as atmospheric pressure. It can be different in different places. Changes in atmospheric pressure are connected to the weather. On a map, a line drawn through places of equal air pressure is called an isobar.

As a pump is used to force more air into a car tyre, the air pushes back with increasing pressure. Due to the extra air, the tyre is also very slightly heavier.

PROJECT: BUILD
AN AIR WEIGHER

WHAT YOU NEED

- thick card
- two plastic cups
- identical balloons
- drawing pins
- glue or tape
- craft knife

1 GLUE A TALL STRIP OF CARD, THE STAND, TO A RECTANGULAR CARD BASE. GLUE SMALL CARD TRIANGLES AT THE JOINT TO KEEP THE STAND UPRIGHT.

2 CUT ANOTHER LONG STRIP OF THICK CARD FOR THE BEAM OF THE BALANCE. CAREFULLY MAKE A SMALL HOLE EXACTLY IN THE MIDDLE OF IT.

3 FIX A PAPER CUP AT EACH END OF THE BALANCE BEAM USING TAPE, GLUE OR DRAWING PINS. MAKE A SMALL HOLE IN THE CENTRE TOP OF THE STAND.

4

5

PUSH A LONG PIN, NAIL OR SIMILAR THROUGH THE HOLES IN THE STAND AND BALANCE BEAM. THE BEAM MUST TILT FREELY. PUT A BALLOON IN EACH CUP.

ENSURE THE BEAM IS EXACTLY LEVEL. IF NECESSARY, ADD TINY WEIGHTS SUCH AS DRAWING PINS OR PAPER CLIPS TO THE SIDE OF THE BEAM WHICH IS HIGHER.

NO LONGER LEVEL

STEADYING THE BALANCE BEAM, REMOVE ONE OF THE BALLOONS FROM ITS CUP. BLOW IT UP AND PUT IT CAREFULLY BACK IN PLACE – AND DOWN GOES THE CUP! BEFORE, THE BALANCE BEAM WAS LEVEL. NOW IT IS NOT, AND THE ONLY DIFFERENCE IS THE AIR IN ONE OF THE BALLOONS.

EXTRA AIR

Blowing up the balloon forces lots of air into a very limited space. As more air squashes in, it tries harder to get out, and pushes on the inside of the balloon with increasing pressure. There is air pressure inside the other balloon, too, – but it's the same as the normal atmospheric pressure outside.

EQUAL AIR PRESSURE OUTSIDE AND INSIDE

GREATER AIR PRESSURE INSIDE

PARTLY BLOW UP THE OTHER BALLOON. DOES THE BALANCE BEAM TIP DOWN LESS?

PAPER WEIGHT

Smooth a sheet of newspaper over a ruler which has one end over-hanging the table. Quickly hit the ruler's end. It is mostly the weight of the air that stops the paper rising.

TRY LARGE AND SMALL SHEETS, SMOOTHED DOWN CAREFULLY. WHICH MOVES LEAST?

AIR PRESSURE

RULER

NEWSPAPER

MEASURING AIR PRESSURE

The air all around presses on us and everything else, with a force called atmospheric pressure. This pressure does not stay the same. Changes in atmospheric pressure are linked to the weather. A barometer measures changes in atmospheric pressure to help us forecast the weather.

PROJECT: BUILD A BAROMETER

Barometers are used on ships to warn of high winds and storms.

BAROMETER

CUT OUT AND STRETCH A PIECE OF BALLOON OVER THE JAR. TAPE IT FIRMLY TO THE RIM.

TAPE ONE END OF THE DRINKING STRAW TO THE CENTRE OF THE BALLOON CIRCLE.

TAPE A STRAIGHTENED PAPER CLIP TO THE FREE END OF THE DRINKING STRAW. CUT AN UPRIGHT SLIT IN ONE SIDE OF THE BOX AND MARK EVENLY SPACED LINES ALONG IT. PUT THE JAR IN THE BOX, PAPER CLIP POKING THROUGH THE SLIT. BEND THE END OF THE PAPER CLIP TO MAKE A POINTER OVER THE MARKS.

WHAT YOU NEED

- jam jar
- balloon
- drinking straw
- paper clip
- cardboard box
- tape
- scissors

CORRECT
PLACE
PUT YOUR
BAROMETER WHERE
THE TEMPERATURE
STAYS THE SAME,
SUCH AS A CELLAR
OR AIRING
CUPBOARD. LOOK
AT THE POINTER AT
THE SAME TIME
DAILY. IT SHOULD
RISE AND FALL AS
THE WEATHER
CHANGES.

HIGHS AND LOWS

As atmospheric pressure outside increases, it squashes the air in the jar by pressing on the balloon, making the pointer rise. When atmospheric pressure falls, the jar's air pressure is now relatively higher, so it bulges the balloon and tilts the pointer down. High atmospheric pressure usually brings calm, settled, clear weather. Low pressure often means clouds, wind, and rain.

POINTER

JAR

HIGHER ATMOSPHERIC PRESSURE

LOWER ATMOSPHERIC PRESSURE

POINTER RISES

POINTER FALLS

THERMOMETER

If you take your barometer from a cool place to a warm one, for a short time it becomes a thermometer instead. The heat makes the air in the jar get bigger or expand, so the pointer falls. This is why you need to keep the barometer at a constant temperature to measure the slow changes in air pressure accurately.

COOL AIR

WARM AIR

FLOATING ON AIR

As a fan or propeller turns, it pulls air in from one side and pushes it out the other. If the fan faces up, it pushes air down and provides a lifting force. The hovercraft uses this method to trap high-pressure air beneath and lift itself just above the ground. It 'floats on air' over land or water.

Hovercraft have main lifting fans in their bodies and separate propellers to push themselves along.

PROJECT: BUILD A HOVERCRAFT

HOVERCRAFT

MAKE A HOLE WITH A PENCIL IN A SMALL SQUARE OF CARD.

GLUE THE CARD TO THE POLYSTYRENE PLATE, IN THE MIDDLE OF THE UNDERSIDE. PUSH A PENCIL THROUGH THE CARD HOLE AND PLATE TO MAKE A WIDER HOLE.

PUSH THE NECK OF THE BALLOON FROM THE UNDERSIDE THROUGH BOTH HOLES.

WHAT YOU NEED

- polystyrene plate
- balloon
- stiff card
- glue
- pencil

TRAPPED!

The high-pressure air rushing out of the balloon is like air being pushed down by a hovercraft's fan. It flows into the space below the plate and gets partly trapped by the plate's rim, which is like the hovercraft's flexible rubber 'skirt'. Air pressure rises underneath until it is enough to lift the craft slightly. As air flows out around the rim, more air rushes in from the balloon to keep up the pressure.

VERY HIGH AIR PRESSURE INSIDE BALLOON

LIFTING FORCE

LIFTING FORCE

ESCAPING AIR

HIGH AIR PRESSURE UNDER CRAFT

ESCAPING AIR

GOING FORWARDS

Try cutting a small V-shaped notch in the rim of the plate, and then set your hovercraft going again. Does the extra air blowing out of this notch cause a pushing force that makes the hovercraft travel in a certain direction?

SEE WHAT HAPPENS WHEN YOU PLACE A FEW SMALL LUMPS OF MODELLING CLAY EVENLY AROUND THE PLATE TO INCREASE ITS WEIGHT. DOES IT HOVER AS EASILY?

WHEN AIR PUSHES BACK

Parachutes have a large area designed to force aside lots of air. This means a large air resistance, so they drift down slowly.

As you walk along, you push air out of the way. You rarely notice – but if you run fast, you push air out of the way more quickly, and you feel this as 'wind' on your face. The bigger an object is and the faster it moves, the more air it must push aside. The air pushes back with a force called air or wind resistance.

PROJECT: TEST WIND RESISTANCE

WIND TESTER

WHAT YOU NEED

- two identical toy cars
- length of stiff cardboard
- two thin lengths of cardboard
- paper
- tape
- electric fan
- scissors

USING TWO SAME-SIZED PAPER RECTANGLES, TAPE ONE EDGE TO THE FRONT OF EACH CAR. ON ONE CAR, BEND THE PAPER TO FORM A SMOOTH CURVE. ON THE OTHER, FOLD THE PAPER INTO A FLAT FRONT. TAPE THE REAR EDGES TO THE CARS.

GLUE THIN CARD STRIPS TO A STIFF BOARD, AS EDGES FOR THE RACETRACK. RAISE THE TRACK AT ONE END ON BOOKS FOR A GENTLE SLOPE. PLACE THE ELECTRIC FAN AT THE BOTTOM IN THE CENTRE OF THE TRACK TO CREATE A 'WIND'.

READY STEADY GO!
RELEASE THE CARS FROM THE TOP OF THE SLOPE AT EXACTLY THE SAME TIME. WHICH ONE ROLLS DOWN FASTEST? (IF BOTH GATHER SPEED TOO QUICKLY, LOWER THE RAISED END OF THE BOARD TO MAKE THE SLOPE MORE SHALLOW.) SWAP THE PAPER SHAPES FROM ONE CAR TO THE OTHER AND TEST THEM AGAIN.

WHAT A DRAG

As each car moves along, it forces its way against the air or 'wind' from the fan. This air slips easily over the car with the curved paper. But it hits the car with the flat front with greater force and creates much more resistance. So this car travels slower. The slowing effect of air or wind resistance is known as drag. A smoothly widening curve that causes least drag is known as a streamlined shape.

MOVING AIR HITS BROAD FRONT

GREATER AIR RESISTANCE

MOVING AIR SLIDES EASILY OVER SMOOTH CURVE

LESS AIR RESISTANCE

NOSE CONES

Try different streamlined paper shapes on the two cars, like a V or a 'nose-cone'.

LOOK AT THE SHAPES OF FAST CARS, BOATS, AND PLANES. SEE HOW THEY ARE STREAMLINED TO REDUCE AIR RESISTANCE OR DRAG.

HOW AIR FLOWS

When designers test new shapes of cars, boats, planes, bridges, and skyscrapers, they often use a wind tunnel. This blows air past the object at high speed and shows the flow by ribbons, smoke or streamers. It helps designers to create faster cars that use less fuel, and structures that are safer.

PROJECT: BUILD A WIND TUNNEL

Airflow over a car shows the amount of wind resistance or drag. The lower this becomes, the less fuel the car uses.

WIND TUNNEL

WHAT YOU NEED

- cardboard box lid
- two stiff card triangles
- four paper clips
- ribbon or tissue paper
- thin string
- glue
- scissors
- electric fan
- card tube

CUT A RECTANGLE SHAPE FROM THE MIDDLE OF THE BOX LID TO LEAVE A STRONG FRAME.

GLUE TWO LARGE CARD TRIANGLES TO THE BOTTOM OF THE SIDES, TO MAKE A FIRM BASE.

PUSH PAPER CLIPS ON TO THE FRAME EDGES. JOIN OPPOSING PAIRS OF PAPER CLIPS WITH THIN STRING STRETCHED FAIRLY TIGHT.

WRAP ONE END OF A RIBBON AROUND THE MIDDLE OF EACH STRING AND GLUE OR TAPE IT FIRMLY IN PLACE.

SHOW THE FLOW

As the 'wind' from the electric fan goes past the test shape, it changes in direction. It blows the ribbons or tissue-paper strips with it, to show its pattern of flow. If the ribbons extend smoothly, this indicates a steady flow. If they flutter greatly, this shows a faster or more irregular pattern. Often the air swirls around just past the test shape, in a whirlpool-like area called a vortex. For a fast vehicle like a racing car, this would cause drag and make the car slower.

AIR FLOW

TEST SHAPE

AIR FLOW

TESTING TIME
TAPE THE TEST SHAPE, SUCH AS A CARD TUBE, TO A PENCIL AND HOLD ACROSS THE MIDDLE OF THE FRAME. MOVE THE PAPER CLIPS UNTIL THE RIBBONS ARE JUST ABOVE AND BELOW IT. FROM THE SIDE, AIM THE ELECTRIC FAN AT THE MIDDLE OF THE SHAPE. SWITCH ON — AND SEE THE RIBBONS FLUTTER IN THE BREEZE!

MORE SHAPES

Try different test shapes like a long box and a long triangle. Which has the smoothest airflow?

TRY THE WING SHAPE FROM PAGE 22. CAN YOU SEE THE UPPER RIBBON FLUTTERING FASTER THAN THE LOWER ONE?

USING THE WIND

Anything that moves has a type of energy known as kinetic energy. Wind is moving air. We can catch its energy to use in many ways – from sails on boats and windsurfers, to wind-mills that work machines, and wind turbines that generate electricity.

A windsurfer sail has stiff strips, battens, to curve it like a plane's wing (see opposite).

PROJECT: BUILD A LANDYACHT

LANDYACHT

WHAT YOU NEED

- thick card
- drinking straws
- cotton reels
- paper
- bottle cap
- paper clips
- paper-fasteners
- cotton thread
- drawing pin
- tape
- glue
- modelling clay
- scissors
- craft knife
- electric fan

1 CUT THE YACHT'S BASE FROM STIFF CARD. TAPE A STRAW TO THE REAR UNDERSIDE OF THE BASE FOR THE BACK AXLE.

2 STRAIGHTEN A PAPER CLIP, BEND IT IN HALF, THEN BEND THE ENDS OUTWARDS TO MAKE A T. GLUE IT TO THE STRAW FOR THE BOOM.

3 TAPE THE STRAIGHT ENDS OF THE PAPER CLIP NEAR ONE END OF ANOTHER STRAW, WHICH WILL BE THE MAST.

4 MAKE A SMALL HOLE IN THE MIDDLE OF THE BASE. INSERT THE LOWER END OF THE MAST. FASTEN IT UNDERNEATH WITH ANOTHER T-SHAPED PAPER CLIP.

5 CUT A TRIANGLE OF PAPER FOR THE SAIL. GLUE ONE EDGE ALONG THE MAST.

6 GLUE OR TAPE THE SAIL'S LOWER CORNER TO THE BOOM END. GIVE THE SAIL A SLIGHT CURVE.

7

PUSH A COTTON REEL ON TO EACH END OF THE BACK AXLE. SECURE WITH PAPER FASTENERS.

8

PUSH A SHORTER LENGTH OF STRAW THROUGH A COTTON REEL AS A FRONT AXLE. TAPE THE STRAW UNDER THE BASE BETWEEN THE FRONT FORKS. GLUE A BOTTLE CAP TO THE BACK OF THE BASE. ATTACH COTTON THREAD FROM THE BOOM END TO A DRAWING PIN IN THE REAR OF THE BASE.

SAIL ON WHEELS

The 'wind' from the fan pushes against the sail's large surface. This gives the sail a force in the same direction as the wind. But the landyacht cannot roll easily in this direction due to its reel wheels. However, it can use part of the force to roll forwards. Experiment with different wind directions and varying the length of cotton thread to the boom's end.

COTTON THREAD

BACK AXLE

SAIL

BALLAST

MAST

BOOM

FRONT FORKS

PAPER CLIPS SECURE BOOM AND MAST

PAPER-FASTENER SECURES WHEEL

MOVEMENT

WIND

GONE WITH THE WIND

PUT A BALL OF MODELLING CLAY INTO THE BOTTLE CAP TO WORK AS A BALLAST WEIGHT 'SAILOR' AND STOP THE LANDYACHT TIPPING OVER! ON A VERY SMOOTH FLOOR, USE AN ELECTRIC FAN TO BLOW THE LANDYACHT ALONG.

AGAINST THE WIND

The sail's curved shape works like a plane wing (see next page). Wind passing over the sail creates lower air pressure in front of the sail and 'sucks' in this direction. Part of this force makes the yacht roll, even into the wind, which sailors call 'tacking'.

TRY TO 'TACK' IN A ZIG-ZAG UPWIND.

FORCE

SAIL

MOVEMENT

WIND

FLYING HIGH

Pelicans glide far without flapping, relying on their curved wing shape.

Birds, bees, and bats do it, and so do some people – fly through the air. Of course, we need planes. But a plane wing works in a similar way to a bird wing. The secret is the way that air flows over the wing's curved shape, known as an aerofoil, to produce the upward force called lift.

PROJECT: BUILD A MODEL GLIDER

In the late 1870s, Otto Lilienthal was first to design and fly gliders with arched aerofoil-type wings.

MODEL GLIDER

WHAT YOU NEED

- thin card
- drinking straws
- modelling clay
- glue
- tape
- scissors

1 FOLD A LONG CARD RECTANGLE IN HALF LENGTHWAYS FOR THE WING. GLUE A STRAW INTO THE FOLD. KEEPING THE LOWER SURFACE FLAT, PUSH THE UPPER SURFACE TO MAKE IT SLIGHTLY 'HUMPED'. GLUE THE EDGES.

2 GLUE ANOTHER STRAW TO THE WING AT RIGHT ANGLES. PLACE IT ON THE FLAT UNDERSIDE, IN THE MIDDLE OF THE WING. ENSURE THE WING IS NEAR ONE END OF THE STRAW, LEAVING A SHORT 'NOSE'.

3 FOLD A SMALLER STRIP OF CARD IN HALF, THEN FOLD EACH OF THE HALVES IN HALF AGAIN, TO MAKE A W SHAPE. GLUE THE MIDDLE TWO SECTIONS TO MAKE THE T-SHAPED FIN (TAIL) AND REAR WINGS.

GETTING A LIFT

Air flowing past the wing must travel farther over the curved upper surface than under the flat lower surface. So this upper air moves faster – and faster-moving air creates lower air pressure. The relatively higher air pressure under the wing pushes the wing and whole glider up, with a force called lift. This helps your glider to stay in the air longer.

FASTER-MOVING AIR OVER TOP

LIFT

AEROFOIL CURVE

SLOWER-MOVING AIR ALONG UNDERSIDE

WING GOES FORWARDS

TEST FLIGHTS

Your craft is a glider – a plane with no engine. In windless conditions launch it gently, aiming slightly down. If it nose-dives, remove part of the counterweight. If it swoops up and then dives, called stalling, add more weight. Keep adjusting until the glider flies smoothly in a shallow downward path.

4

TAPE THE T-SHAPE TO THE LONGER END OF THE STRAW. PRESS A PIECE OF MODELLING CLAY TO THE NOSE END AS A COUNTERWEIGHT, AND PREPARE FOR TAKE-OFF!

SPANS AND SHAPES

Test wings of different lengths (span) and different distances from front to back (chord). Can you work out why real gliders have very long, narrow wings? (See next page.)

LAUNCH THE GLIDER IN DIFFERENT WAYS – FAST, SLOW, SLIGHTLY UP, OR BANKED (TILTED TO ONE SIDE).

CONTROL IN THE AIR

The first fully controlled, powered, heavier-than-air flying machine – a plane – was the Wright brothers' *Flyer* in 1903.

Balloons drift with the wind. But planes can turn in different directions, and climb and dive, because they have moveable panels on their wings and tail, called control surfaces.

PROJECT: ADD AILERONS

TO THE GLIDER

A glider has ailerons, or moveable flaps, on its wings. These help the glider to tilt, bank, and turn.

AILERONS

WHAT YOU NEED

- thin card
- tape or glue
- scissors

1

TAPE EQUAL-SIZED CARD STRIPS TO THE OUTER REAR EDGES OF THE WINGS ON YOUR GLIDER (SEE PREVIOUS PAGE).

2

BEND ONE OF THE CARD AILERONS DOWN VERY SLIGHTLY AND THE OTHER ONE UP.

LIFT OR LOWER?

If the aileron angles downwards, it alters the air flow over the aerofoil shape and increases the force of lift. Also air coming off the bottom of the wing pushes on the aileron and forces it up. The combined effect is to raise the wing tip, so the plane tilts or banks away from that side. With the aileron pointing up, the reverse happens and the wing tip is lowered.

LIFT FROM WING

MORE LIFT FROM WING

MAIN AIR FLOW

BANKING AROUND

AILERONS ARE CONTROL SURFACES AT THE REAR OF THE WING TIPS. THEY CHANGE THE FLOW OF AIR TO MAKE ONE TIP RISE AND THE OTHER FALL SLIGHTLY. THIS MAKES THE GLIDER BANK TO ONE SIDE AND SO ITS PATH TENDS TO CURVE OR TURN AROUND IN A CIRCLE. THE MORE THE AILERONS ARE ANGLED, THE STEEPER THE BANK AND THE TIGHTER THE TURN.

MORE CONTROL

Tape a card strip to the rear of the glider's fin (tail). This control surface is called a rudder. With ailerons straight (not angled), bend the rudder slightly to one side and see how the glider flies.

ANGLE THE AILERON UP, ON THE SIDE TO WHICH THE RUDDER IS BENT. DOES THE GLIDER TURN TIGHTER?

WINGS IN A SPIN

The forward motion of a plane's wings through the air creates lift (see previous page). Another method is to spin the wing around. It still creates lift, in the same way – but the craft does not have to move forwards. This is how a helicopter flies.

Autogyros have unpowered rotors that spin in the air flow as they move forwards.

The helicopter's rotors or blades are really long, thin, wings that spin around, or rotate.

PROJECT: BUILD A HELISPINNER

HELISPINNER

WHAT YOU NEED

- paper
- drinking straw
- thin dowel
- modelling clay
- glue
- tape
- scissors

MAKE TWO SMALL 'HALF-WINGS' AS SHOWN ON PAGES 22–23. GLUE THEM TO ONE STRAW, FACING OPPOSITE DIRECTIONS.

FIRMLY TAPE THE SMALL DOWEL TO THE MIDDLE OF THE STRAW.

STICK A PIECE OF MODELLING CLAY ON TO THE LOWER END OF THE DOWEL TO ACT AS A COUNTERWEIGHT.

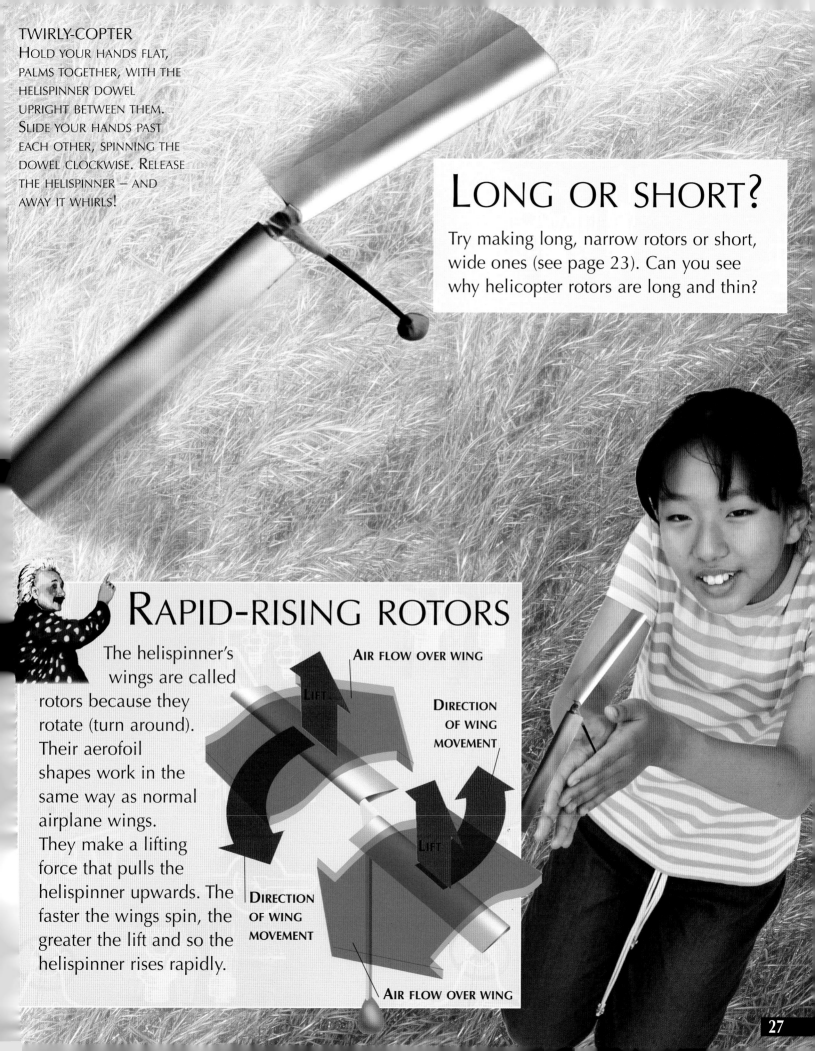

TWIRLY-COPTER

HOLD YOUR HANDS FLAT, PALMS TOGETHER, WITH THE HELISPINNER DOWEL UPRIGHT BETWEEN THEM. SLIDE YOUR HANDS PAST EACH OTHER, SPINNING THE DOWEL CLOCKWISE. RELEASE THE HELISPINNER – AND AWAY IT WHIRLS!

LONG OR SHORT?

Try making long, narrow rotors or short, wide ones (see page 23). Can you see why helicopter rotors are long and thin?

RAPID-RISING ROTORS

The helispinner's wings are called rotors because they rotate (turn around). Their aerofoil shapes work in the same way as normal airplane wings. They make a lifting force that pulls the helispinner upwards. The faster the wings spin, the greater the lift and so the helispinner rises rapidly.

AIR FLOW OVER WING

LIFT

DIRECTION OF WING MOVEMENT

DIRECTION OF WING MOVEMENT

LIFT

AIR FLOW OVER WING

AIR, ENERGY, AND POWER

Many turbines together are known as a wind farm.

The whirling blades of wind turbines are seen on hillsides around the world. These machines change the kinetic energy of moving air (see page 20) into the energy of electricity. They help our quest for non-polluting, sustainable power.

PROJECT: BUILD A WIND TURBINE

WIND TURBINE

WHAT YOU NEED

- **plastic bottle**
- **cardboard tube**
- **thin card**
- **drinking straws**
- **thick card**
- **beads**
- **paper clips**
- **string**
- **glue**
- **tape**
- **scissors**

1 GLUE TWO 'HALF-WINGS' (SEE PAGE 26) TO A STRAW. POINT THEM THE SAME WAY, BUT WITH CURVED SURFACES OPPOSITE.

STRAIGHTEN A PAPER CLIP, BEND IT IN HALF AND THEN BEND THE ENDS TO FORM A T SHAPE (SEE PAGE 20). TAPE THE FREE ENDS TO THE MIDDLE OF THE STRAW JOINING THE HALF-WINGS, WHICH ARE THE TURBINE BLADES.

CAREFULLY MAKE A HOLE JUST BIG ENOUGH FOR A STRAW IN THE BOTTOM OF THE PLASTIC BOTTLE, AND A SIMILAR HOLE IN ITS CAP. PUSH A LONG STRAW THROUGH THE HOLES AND FIT A BEAD OVER EACH END. THIS STRAW IS THE DRIVE SHAFT.

2 FIX THE BLADES TO THE SHAFT BY GLUING THE CENTRAL PART OF THE PAPER CLIP INTO THE END OF THE STRAW AT THE CAP.

3 MAKE A TALL TUBE TOWER AND WIDE BASE FROM CARD. TRIM THE TUBE TOP TO FIT THE PLASTIC BOTTLE AND GLUE THIS ON.

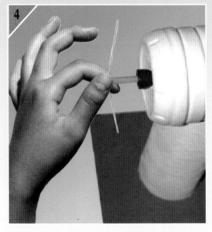

4 BEND ANOTHER PAPER CLIP INTO A T SHAPE. GLUE THIS INTO THE OTHER END OF THE SHAFT.

5 BEND THE PAPER CLIP'S ENDS INTO V-SHAPED HOOKS. TIE ONE END OF THE COTTON TO ONE V AND THE OTHER END TO A BEAD.

WIND WORK

The rotor blades of the turbine work like plane wings, each creating a lifting force at its curved surface. This force does not actually lift the blade. It 'sucks' it round in a circle, making the drive shaft turn. The two rotor blades work together since their curved surfaces face opposite ways, and so their lifting forces give the same turning motion.

CURVED SURFACE FACES DOWN

DRIVE SHAFT SPINS

AIR FLOW

LIFT

WEIGHT RISES

TOWER

AIR FLOW

CURVED SURFACE FACES UP

BASE

WHEN WIND WINDS

PLACE THE WIND TURBINE IN A WINDY PLACE, OR BLOW AN ELECTRIC FAN AT IT. (PUT WEIGHTS ON THE BASE IF NEEDED TO HOLD IT STILL.) THE BLADES BEGIN TO WHIRL AND TURN THE DRIVE SHAFT. THIS WINDS THE COTTON AROUND THE HOOKS AND RAISES THE BEAD. THE WIND'S ENERGY IS MADE INTO TURNING ENERGY, WHICH IS USED TO LIFT THE BEAD WEIGHT.

BLADE SHAPES

Try making another set of rotors, but this time glue them at angle to each other on the straw, like the blades of a fan. Is this version of the turbine more powerful?

FOR THESE ANGLED ROTORS, DOES IT MATTER IF THE CURVED (AEROFOIL) SURFACE OF EACH BLADE FACES FORWARDS, OR THE FLAT SURFACE?

29

AIR HISTORY

About 520 BC In Ancient Greece, scientist and thinker Anaximenes suggested that air was a 'primary substance' which could be turned into other substances and materials.

335 BC Aristotle described how air was one of the four 'elements' from which all other substances and materials were made, the other three being fire, water, and earth. These views lasted almost 2,000 years.

1620 Jan Baptista van Helmont suspected that air was not a single pure substance but a mixture of different substances, which he named gases.

1643 Evangelista Torricelli made an early version of the barometer and said that air was a real substance with weight.

1674 John Mayow reported that a candle in a sealed jar used up part of the air as it burned, and a mouse in the jar did the same. He stated that air contained 'nitro-aerial spirit' needed for burning and breathing.

1772 Several scientists, including Karl Scheele, discovered a gas in air which was later called nitrogen.

1774 Joseph Priestly discovered a gas that made a candle burn extra-bright. He told colleague Antoine Lavoisier, who worked out that air was one-fifth oxygen, needed for burning, and breathing, and four-fifths 'azote' ('no life'), later renamed nitrogen.

1783 Joseph-Michael and Jacques-Etienne Montgolfier made the first hot-air balloon. Later that year Jean Pilatre de Rozier and Francois Laurent (Marquis d'Arlandes) made the first balloon flight.

1884 Sir James Dewar showed how air could be turned into a liquid, following research by Szygmunt Wroblewski and Karol Olszewski.

1890s William Ramsay proved that air contained tiny amounts of other gases. We now know these as argon, helium, krypton, xenon, neon, and radon.

1902 The first practical airship and the first air-conditioner were made.

1903 Orville Wright made the first true airplane flight, in the *Flyer* designed and built by himself and brother Wilbur.

1985 Scientists first measured loss of ozone (O_3), a form of oxygen in air, which led to the 'ozone hole' in the atmosphere that lets the Sun's harmful radiation through.

GLOSSARY

Anemometer A device that measures the speed of wind.

Atmosphere The layer of air around the Earth, which becomes less dense with height.

Atom The smallest piece or particle of a pure substance (chemical element).

Barometer A device that measures the pressure of air.

Density The amount of matter of a substance, usually measured as mass or weight, in a certain volume.

Drag The force pushing against an object as it travels through a fluid, as when air pushes back on a car.

Fluid A substance that can flow, including liquids like water, and gases like those in air.

Gas A substance that can flow, and which can change volume to fill its container completely.

Isobar The line on a weather map that joins places of equal atmospheric pressure.

Kinetic energy The energy possessed by an object or substance due to its having movement or motion.

Lift A force created by the wing shape called the aerofoil, which lifts a plane upwards.

Meteorology The study of the atmosphere, especially the processes and events of weather and climate.

Molecules Two or more atoms joined together, to make the smallest pieces or particles of most everyday substances and materials.

Pressure Pushing or pressing force measured over a certain area.

Thermometer A device that measures temperature, or the amount of heat energy in a substance or object.

Wind resistance The force pushing against an object that tries to move through air or against the wind.

Wind vane A broad surface that can swivel around, to show the direction in which the wind blows.

INDEX